When the World Walks Toward You

# When the World Walks Toward You

Poems by

Myra Shapiro

Cover design by Shay Culligan
Front cover artwork: "Strange Birds" by Josh Dorman

ISBN: 978-1-63980-020-9

Kelsay Books
502 South 1040 East, A-119
American Fork, Utah  84003
Kelsaybooks.com

For
community

To my family and friends
artists all
with whom
I play, sing, laugh and write

# Also by Myra Shapiro

*I'll See You Thursday* (poems)
*Four Sublets: Becoming a Poet in New York* (memoir)
*In Greenwich Village We Talk of Love* (chapbook)
*12 Floors Above the Earth* (poems)

# Acknowledgments

Special thanks to the editors of the following publications where these poems, some of which have been revised, first appeared.

*Bellevue Literary Review:* "The Dreamer"
*Gyroscope Review:* "Out of the Kitchen"
*Moment Magazine & LIPS:* "Borscht"
*Nimrod:* "Dearth," "The Letter *d*"
*Passager:* "Ode to Elsewhere"
*Paterson Literary Review:* "*Chenille*/Caterpillar/Chenille"
*Rattapallax:* "For Nazim Hikmet in the Old Prison Now a Four Seasons Hotel"
*Rattle:* "In a Room at the Marriott Marquis," "The Alteration of Love"
*River Styx:* "Gaza," "Put the Kettle On," (International Poetry Contest Winner, 2014), "The Faces of Women"
*Spillway:* "When the World Walks Toward You"
*The Comstock Review:* "If Martha Graham Can Die," "Living in the Pages"
*The New Yorker:* "These Are the Pearls"
*Upstreet:* "At the Frick"

Anthologies:
*Like Light:* "The Knotted Handkerchief"
*Muse Matrix:* "Zelda"
*Speaking for my Self:* "The Bouquet," "Lake Damariscotta," "At the End of the Play"
*Verse-virtual:* "The Alteration of Love"
*The Best American Poetry:* "For Nazim Hikmet in the Old Prison Now a Four Seasons Hotel"

Deep gratitude to Susan Weiman for her advice and organizational/administrative assistance.

# Contents

"What was *was,* deal the cards."
—Ida Stein

"What we have loved is with us ever,
ever, ever!
So you are with me far into the past . . ."
—Robert Bly

I

# If Martha Graham Can Die


so can I. I
remember, at her death,
those words coming, an inkling
of what lay ahead:
I was going to die.

Not my mother's death—
she'd disappeared, yes,
but she wasn't
        Martha Graham

telling me *there is only one of you*
*for all time*

and those words
stayed.
      In utero
I was the egg
with will so strong
death was
       inconceivable.

How elegant that word
*inconceivable*
arriving as I write—
           death

to be conceived
      breath by breath
           leading me on

# When the World Walks Toward You


Throw a word into the room
   And see where it goes. To
The heart, the haunt, to the hearth
   On fire. My mother
Sings of tulips; father is a big red rose.
   Breathe in
Her chicken soup simmering on the stove.
   My favorite haunt
Has chicken soup I often order a bowl of.
   What haunted my mother
Was flirting with the surgeon before her daughter died
   And I was born—other
Wise I wouldn't be here—with my daughter
   To light a fire
When winter comes—no lack
   Of kindling
Shipped from L. L. Bean.
   Ashes cost.
They look like snow. I look like my father.
   My younger sister sings
Like mother. Mockingbirds built a nest
   In the chimney
This spring. Beside the grate
   We found a fledgling dead.
There's a commotion in my hearth all mother long.

# Lake Damariscotta

And the lake said, "I am a table."
And the trees said, "I'll surround you."
And the island said, "I'll be the centerpiece."

And I said, "May I sit?"
And I asked, "What will you serve?"

And the fish wouldn't answer
And the sun began to leave

But the waves took pity
And said *memory.*

# On Time

I. History

A piece of life. A chip
between the stones
in the arch of Washington Square

or a jagged green piece
of Union Square where my family
rallied for unions. Slip me in. Place me there.


II. Story

I want my life to be a story. With chapters. Chapter one would say
an 11-year-old sister died the year I was born. I couldn't be quiet. I
couldn't be exchanged. I fought on the playground and made myself
heard in school. Later from the back seat of cars I learned to play
nice and marry a prince (says my mother, who had lost a princess).
Daughters come. My husband thrives while I struggle in suburbia.
Next comes the miracle—it's a story of joy after all—the Women's
Movement to alter time. I can go anywhere. All the way back to
New York City. The children grow up and out. My husband stays.
Life fits. Poetry fills the pages. But there exists a foreshadowing
(every story has an ending).

III. Poetry

One day as I lead a class in poetic forms
two women enter, waves
to the shore. One wears a tag: *Marina.* The other,
fetching, younger one:
*Tsipora.* "Shall I spell it for you?"
she asks. My sister, her
name! "Sorry we're late."
Walking into my class one day
       death just like that.

# In Bright Green She Leaves

I take the Long Island Rail Road,
the 12:09 to Pinelawn,
where on Sunday
a bus meets the train for the cemetery
> The New Montefiore Cemetery
> opened in 1927

less than an hour from the City.
It is the site of my sister's grave.

Click on locator. There are four with her name; they are
85 years, 78 years, 87 years
and 11, yes 11. In June 1931 (before I came) they found a space.
They had to. The surgeon said. . .

It has always been unspoken. No one goes there.
In my bottom drawer

> 1 navy rayon jumper
> 1 still life of flowers
> 2 paint boxes father's hers
> 1 lined tablet

> An index card with the name of where she is

this fall of 2016 I want to
see it, the space. I must move slowly—
"You can't go to it," the man says,
"too many dried stumps, clumped roots blocking the pathway."

I *will* / push
between bushes wedged
against stones and over
limbs and brokenness.

My body remembers the motion.
"There it is," he says. I see
a tiny space. Nothing
to mark it? *There*
*it is,* he repeats.
And in front of my eyes

                    her name

                              it stands deeply cut
                              from 80 years ago
                              polished stone
                              like new, and tall
                              4 feet tall and thin,
                              only the lover
                              of flowers would
                              place there. Only
                              my father would.

             Only my father would.
             Only a lover of beauty
             Would lift my words
             To stand like her stone
             In the New Montefiore
             Cemetery where she is
             In a space held by the
             International Workers
             Order. Order is what
             One makes to go on
             Living when death is
             The life you have
             To live with. You must
             Create a stone to say
             Shirley Stein. Here

                    23

We will know she lived
Painting flowers. Here
He has ordered leaves
To rise from her name.

# The Dreamer

To escape a dying empire czars strolled
       along a promenade in Nice.

My father took that scene to heart—he dreamed
       of being king for sixty years.

Hiding in a rain barrel to cross the Russian border,
       riding steerage on the ocean

to arrive in New York City, he peddled
       south to Dalton, Georgia,

and never lost the dream. When at last his shop was closed,
       he found a hi-rise next to Biscayne Bay,

announcing *here* was peace—could we doubt palms
       swaying near the sea?

The week he died I had to drive through palm trees
       to his side.

The Chapel faced the sea. The moon over Miami
       spread her *creme*

for his dessert. She serves it to him still.

# Ode to Elsewhere

When I was six or seven
my mother arranged piano lessons.
We had no piano; a keyboard
made of cardboard was to do
Mozart.

After school I practiced for a year
playing notes without a sound
to learn what, in this land of milk
and honey, she aspired to: Beauty.
Culture.

At dinner my father forbid us
to talk. There was news
to listen to on the radio. A war
was going on. The world, it was
elsewhere.

My parents came from there:
a place charged with flight—
from which I set out to make
matchless music.

# *Chenille*//Caterpillar//Chenille

*for N. T. who asked*

In the avocado green of a kitchen,
a 50s marriage, children,
           I wanted wings, I wanted Paris

so I breathed my father in: traveling salesman,
        dogged immigrant's
           inch by inch, he traveled a whole family

to a distant state:
        1940 Deep South
           where a lady named Mizz Evans invented chenille

pulling cotton tufts through fabric, chenille
        from the single needle
           of her sewing machine, chenille

for something new, a surge of yarns, a woman
        scissoring the threads
           *chenille*—French word spreading across our beds—

rolling hills she hung on a line so everyone could see
        and want it, chenille
           from which my father made a living

during the Depression—
        in Dalton, Georgia
           *The Bedspread Center of the World.*

# Out of the Kitchen

Once I watched Julia Child
form a tray for hors d'oeuvres
from a bread she'd pulled
the insides out of. It was her art,
it was her voice

her laughter when a chicken slipped
from her hands, her aplomb
lifting the fallen fowl, and with gusty
assurance, making herself
a person to relish

that we remember. The sound of her
made us cook a chicken-
in-a-pot, if only to jolly our lives,
if only to lift ourselves
out of the kitchen.

# Anecdote of the Deck

*It did not give of bird or bush,*
*Like nothing else in Tennessee.*
    —Wallace Stevens

The fichus is propped in a white ceramic pot on the deck. Its leaves catch light; they have that winsome, come-to-me nature. Standing in the woods beyond the deck are hickory trees and pines, an oafy, flat-leafed hornbeam and the tall skeleton of an elm. At the v of the deck is the queen, a magnolia whose history through fall and winter into spring, I've recorded from the closeness of a chair. I'd like to feel at home here. Mostly, my efforts have been failures. To be fair to myself I'm a newcomer out-of-doors so when I build the deck with cherry wood and have it painted, I don't know how much raw sweetness will be lost. Or that blue will jar you when you first come out. Beyond the deck everything is good—the trees, the underbrush, everything except the run-down wire fence closing in the yard. We strung it for the German Shepherd my husband bought, and it's as sad as the dog was. Pal we named him. I'd wanted the kids to have a pet to make life what I'd seen in books. We have two daughters I was trying to fit into Dick and Jane. With Spot named Pal. As you can guess, the story gets messier than any primer would want to say. How my husband had no time for Pal; he'd leave at 7:30 mornings and come home after dark, trying to build his business bigger. How I hated housekeeping in general, much less attending to a dog, so I kept working for the League of Women Voters. We couldn't make Pal fit. When the gas man came to read the meter one November day, the dog ran out the open gate. We announced him missing on Luther's morning show. Whatever happened to him I don't know, but the fence remains to remind me. It's in the foreground of the trees.

# Doppelganger

*for Ciaran Carson, For All We Know*


To be struck by the word *fetch,* the distance a wave travels
From its birth at sea to where it founders on the shore,

The fetch of a journey I'm somehow to be ready for—
The poet has me in his book of poems—

The objects in his lover's life, they're mine: her perfume
*Je Reviens*—my first sophistication—its blue flacon

Still fragrant on my shelf. My watch, an Omega
Bought on shipboard fifty years ago, still ticking.

On my wrist. On hers. Her father/mine
Travels selling linens. When she dies

Driving to Nevers, it rises
In me—the wave

II

# Zelda

A belle, she flung herself outrageously,
the object of every boy's desire.

To the hilt she toyed with them. See her
jump into the pond, naked, *kiss me,*

*double dare you,* in broad daylight.
This way and that she played them forward

for a few light years until she found
the one who soars: he and she,

over the moon, rising—
no matter—through turbulence:

he'll spin while she flails harder—
and what will propel her now?

Italy, France, the Alps, she will
bang her body against

air everywhere, searching for
refuge: one white room

where solidity lives: a bed, a lamp,
a three-shelved bookcase
waiting for her books.

# Living in the Pages

*on reading The Hare with the Amber Eyes, Edmund du Waal*

July 1917. Vienna. 17-year-old Elisabeth Ephrussi, a banker's
daughter, a Jew, is about to enter university.
One of very few women.
Elisabeth is the grandmother of the author.
She is to study philosophy, economics and law.

Ida is in Brooklyn. She will become my mother. She is courted
by a dapper man in Prospect Park. In her new language
she sings *When you wore a tulip*
*and I wore a big red rose.* It is the song of her day.
She is 16, and in one month she will marry my father.

In Vienna it is hot summer. Elisabeth's mother
has a lover. At 38 she will give birth
to a blue-eyed, fair-haired boy.

I must put down my book. A friend is coming at 3.
We'll have tea, and I have new poems he will listen to.

The Austro-Hungarian Empire has just collapsed.

My father, six years before, crossed the Polish border
into Germany. His violin his pillow.

*It takes something to walk out your door and leave everything.*

I haven't eaten breakfast yet. It is late Sunday morning.
Almost March.
My mother always dies in March.

In another 50 pages it will be March 1938.
There are fists at the door.

My friend is coming for poetry.

# She Dances

flamenco. From
the tips of her shoes
to the flutter
of her lashes
her fingers caught
in the ruffles
of her dress
thrusting
above the curve
of her back
our daughter
stamps foot
to floor
to deep-throated
trembling song
her muscles
holding
inquisition
exile.

# The Faces of Women

*". . . men die miserably every day for lack of what is found there."*
—William Carlos Williams

It was the news, the day
leaders of the world gathered
to mourn the writers/ the artists
murdered in Paris.

There are newspapers that refuse
to print the face of a woman.

Reading *The Times* we saw
the mourners in a row: the Israeli
Netanyahu on one end, the Palestinian
Abbas on the other, and in the middle

from Germany Angela Merkel
who was simply erased
in the Orthodox Jewish press.

I am trying to get my head around it. The news

which does not exist.

# Gaza

*"Imagine! Life is normal, with people even free to go to the beach."*
—The NY Times, May 25, 1994

1.

Listen to the beat. Occupation over
it's coming from a drum. Jazzing up the sand.
Beach instead of beachhead. Splash
and wave. Women laughing in the waves
like youngsters rolling in a barrel

when it's not a barricade. Fires
grilling meat in the evening breeze. Words
like *barbecue.* Nice. Ordinary. Letting colors wave
red, black, white and green, letting hours spill,
smelling coffee late into the night: dailiness

taboo for twenty-seven years when, deserted,
under curfew, the beach was nothing more than
wind-smacked shore and wave. Furtively
a woman slipped us flag-colored barrettes
she'd hidden in a bag. That night in Tel Aviv,
same sea, we were mad to go dancing.

Nothing is more serious than pleasure, humans
fully human when we play. Arms and eyes
aimed toward the break of a wave
meeting the shore, delivering shells. Seashells.

2.

I will not go there.
I cannot go
but once women in bright robes
ran along the Mediterranean
laughing and we thought
peace had come.
             I'm on a New York City rooftop
looking out. Don't ask
me to go there.
             I want my life:
my room, my children, their
children, friends to call
or not. I want my room
and the roof. To play
as once I thought
in Gaza women would—
splashing in the waves
when shells came
as seashells. Then the water
was free to wave
frivolously. We rejoiced
and men betrayed us.
Then I was there. Not now.

## Calling You oo oo oo oo oo oo

Circles of air, of sea and wireless take my love to you—
Oh, I am blessed by all the elements, remembering snow in Georgia
falling like confetti when we married so many Februarys ago
and then, 43 years later, again snow falling, though
you are in Aleppo where warm desert winds are blowing
while I am hibernating in New York. When you return we'll tango
on the Rainbow Roof, make toasts for peace, plant peonies
on the patio come spring. Over 60 springs have passed since Ida
in the Bronx delivered me. And Tillie gave you life in Opelika.
We are a gumbo of delicious, disparate parts from the time
we vowed *I do*. O then and now! O me and you!
O world askew!

# At the Jewish Museum

Carl Meyer has hired John Singer Sargent to paint
Mrs. Carl Meyer. Her white Victorian gown
secures the foreground.
Beside her a book stands open, its pages toward us.
Behind her two children lean in
over the settee. Mrs. Meyer's arm reaches to touch
her young son's fingers,
his dark curls a contrast to his white ruffled collar.
By his side his sister
sports a bright pink ribbon in the thickness of her hair.

The year is 1896, the place is London, in the *Spectator:*
"Even Mr. Sargent's skill
has not succeeded in making attractive these over-civilized
European Orientals."

I look again at the exquisite *Mrs. Carl Meyer and Her Children,*
then read again words that led
to the 20th century. "No way," my grandson says.
His father is Muslim, his mother
a Rabbi's grandchild. The words *immigrant*
and *alien* fill our news.
A man smeared his way to The White House
by using them.
A book stands open, its pages toward us.

# For Nazim Hikmet in the Old Prison Now a Four Seasons Hotel

It was from his prison I woke
to the muezzin calling at dawn.
From unbarred windows I saw
six minarets in a brightening sky,
the crescent moon beside Sophia
still there, absolutely
clear in March, the month
my mother always dies,
and I was rising
from fresh sheets to apricots and figs
delivered to our door.
It was his prison
and I couldn't change that.
My bed didn't spring with bugs,
I didn't wait for water
to thaw in the earthen jug:
it ran warm or cold
as I desired. To my touch.
I held his words next to me
  ... *live with the outside,*
  *with its people and animals, struggle and wind—*
    *I mean with the outside beyond the walls.*
  *I mean however and wherever we are,*
  *we must live as if we will never die*

and when the day came
I walked out
into the courtyard
flooded with sun, out
onto the old street, and I could
turn right or left—

I couldn't help it—
walking out on his footprints.

# The Bouquet

Nature frightened me—
you could die from it—
so I stayed in bed
with *A Child's Garden
of Verses,* rescued
from the heaving
and holding breaths
of asthma. Over
and over and
under my covers I read
"The Swing"—
that way I could fly
"up in the air so blue . . ."

Today wind enters my hair
as I walk in a field
of asphodel
and my heart skips
to William Carlos Williams,
his flower, his greeny
word, and I begin
to blabber sweetly to a bug,
"You are lovely
little crawling thing,
I wish I knew your name
so I could write a deeper poem."

My bug keeps crawling. Calling
it lovely gives me Galway,
his milky sow, his blessing
to my mouth. Bless him
for remaining always near.

I wish Emily hadn't
just breezed by—
the buzz of that fly—
to cut me short.

Stevenson must have guessed
up in the air so high
flies never stop on the sky.

# Que Dulce

There's magic in the air. November
Is turning into spring. Such enchantment
Must be love. Que dulce.

The world is growing closer, holding
Two tongues nearer, ringing with the marriage of
Two hemispheres. Que dulce.

!Ariel and Judith! !Judith and Ariel!
The earth has touched the sky, wing and root,
Flight and foot. Que dulce!

My father used to say, *Love
Is not a potato.* He was waiting
For dessert—and here it is.

Que dulce. Que dulce

III

# The Alteration of Love

I was crying—I mean
tears came—about love,
old love, long marriage
spilling past impediments of
who wants what for dinner or
in the bedroom—ins and outs
my father's coarse humor

made a joke of: *you put it in,*
*you pull it out, the story's over,*
(only in Yiddish it rhymed,
words I don't recall). Over,
he is. So is my mother. We
were never to be them.
Now they want me

to stop crying. I was trying
to say something about love—
how one day one of us
will disappear. That's when
my eyes hauled up the sea,
and my mother and father came
to make a child of me.

# There Is a Brother

The tides are out. For miles we walk
on salty grass.
"Watch out," he says—" the sheep
graze all around."

Hand in hand, a guide and I
cross tidal bed.
You must take an other's hand
to build a monument.

"Watch for quicksand, don't stand still."
Barefoot, we walk four miles
to a spire, looming, coming
close, coming closer.

A sister and a brother hand in hand. They're in a picture book I read
in childhood. Or was I reading to my children? Sister, brother
walking to the island of Mont Saint Michel, they've haunted me.
How they lingered, and the tides came in surrounding them, alone,
together on the island. They had to eat, they had to sleep. They had
to make a little life before the tides went out and they would walk
back home.

I do not have a brother. Walking over sand
to that stone island, the guide takes my hand.
After four miles we are there! Mont Saint Michel!

I want to build a life, stranded by the sea,
with my beloved brother next to me.

# At the End of the Play

Twice this month I've cried
at the end of a play, for the men
become disarmed and tender.

It's not Blanche made me weep
in *A Streetcar Named Desire,*
it's the gentleman caller she hoped for
sobbing against the wall.

*In the Next Room,* a new play,
the Victorian doctor's wife asks of him,
 "Make yourself an angel,

open your arms," and, like a child,
he does. In the snow he disrobes
for her. For us. My husband and I

hold his nakedness close
as we walk home—our 57th year
further in than we can climb out of.

"Let's have a brandy," he says.
"Yes, I'd like that," I answer.

# Put the Kettle On

*Tea?* I've begun to ask each evening
partway between dinner and bedtime,
and he's begun to answer *Yes.*

It's an old marriage. We're beginning
to merge. Just this month, arms aching,
I began following his morning routine,
the hot shower so my arms move
with ease. In his case it's knees.
Last night I wanted to sit next to him
as he sat on his side of the bed, simply
to chat a bit about the Middle East,
the peace talks he's been listening to—
and what else was important today?

I wanted to hear his excitement before we went
to our separate sides of the bed,
our particular pillows and the good sleep.
It's all just begun, the new year. March
is here, and we're living it.

# Scrabble

Killing time, the kids gone, we
decided to play Scrabble,
my favorite game, two of us

together in silence. (I read
between turns.) It was his turn
when he said, "I'm tired, let's quit."

My arm
        a grenade
flew across the board—
              broken words
lay on the floor
        little squares of shrapnel
under our table
under the power of my hand.

We were simply playing
Scrabble—he was winning—which I
never mind—it keeps the game
going—but it was late, he was tired.

Well, I had to wake him. I had to
shatter quitting. He said, "I'm
not going to play with you
anymore."

That seemed funny
so I laughed. Then he laughed.
We were young again.

# The Letter *d*

We have been given syllables:
*Or er*

Been witness to mighty creations:
Palmyra, Ephesus

Looked up to stars:
Nelson Eddy singing

*Will you love me ever?*
to Jeannette MacDonald

holding a note
holding us

in May a marriage
and last night

the letter *d*
arrived

inside a dream
inside my passport

a hieroglyph
a link

inviting me to dally
daily—
      listen to the love
      sliding in
breathing life into my letters.

# David: A Blessing

The way our grandson's tongue created
garbled sounds we didn't understand,
a litany toward the candles' light
*Boruch atah adonoy Amen Grandpa*
we heard as praise
letting us know his particular spirit
like everything holy arrives
in mysterious flashes. We laughed.

The authorities called it autism.

# Dervish

Room for many moons
I do not have, no
Room to maneuver.

Do not dwell on it.

Assume the hearse is not
Waiting for me nor the kind
Horse that stops for Emily.

There is replacement
To take place. A knee
To be transformed. And then
What? you ask. To climb

The gangway, cruise
At Christmas time. To
Lo and behold the New Year.

Make room for the kindling.

Kindness allows warmth
To settle in the heart,
To luster there.
This world
Was created for me.
Did I say whirl?
Do I have room to?

# The Knotted Handkerchief

Bruges, the city of lace
I flew to from a dream

when I was turning sixty-three
where who knows what waited

with something to tell me,
mysteriously moves me again.

Back then, at my arrival,
                out the window of my inn,
I saw a statue, Niobe,

filling the canal with her tears,
crying for her dead children.

She was my mother.

It was her grief when she gave birth
to me. Bruges took grief and turned it into art.

This morning I am eighty-three, and
Bruges, in *The NY Times,* has declared itself

a dementia friendly city. In store windows
on display, a knotted handkerchief states

*we want you, please come in*

placed for all who have trouble
remembering why they came.

# In a Room at the Marriott Marquis

To die
in Times Square
is a fact to contemplate
since I am old and here
on 44th Street in a vast hotel
40 floors above the earth

(only there is no earth
visible). Concrete giants
(having gobbled land) stand
planted like Nature.

A shoulder of the Hudson,
a slim body of water,
lies west, and a ferry
is making its way

to the other side, away
from yolk-yellow taxis
in the valley below, where
enormous voices

eager to be heard hawk
*Mama Mia,* TOSHIBA, *Jersey Boys*
*Buy me, Here,* no, *Here, Here!*
and
        tucked in, aslant,
            a radiant red staircase rises
                    to seat you,
                    to fix you
                    like a star—

There is no death! Wake up!

IV

# Arranging the Marriage

Because I wanted to laugh.
              Because these days I cry so
unexpectedly
I wanted to write a poem
              I'd call "The Man I Lug."

              Husband,
it's you, the man I love who can't
        stand or walk.
              Our bed is one-sided.

Caretakers care for you. They stay,
they fill the house.

In another room, in another bed, you are
              armoured: you sleep,
              you eat, no words
              to reveal or joke your way
              through diapers.

Nothing's funny here.

Apart
              what if I rent an apartment
?!

I'm beginning to feel
              the ex
      citement—eating out, then
coming to visit.
     I'd go to museums,
        bring the glow to your bedside.

These nights when I move
      my arm under the pillow—
      one hand finds my other, fingers
waiting
      *hello, stranger*
          to touch

# At the Frick

The old woman stands before *The Lamentation*
*Of Christ* and in it sees her husband, the bent
Neck tilted toward his chest. Absent from
His illness, she has left him with a red-haired
Magdalene devoted to his needs, to his desire
For her fingers through his hair. "Please, your nails
Rake them through my hair"—and she does
Stay hour after hour by his side. Patience
Is difficult for the old woman. Her gift is
To amuse, to travel, to find divinity
In books/ the arts, then bring its story
Home, to pretend there is beauty always
Somewhere that will not end.

# More More More

At 88 what my husband wants
is more. Yesterday

here's what came FedEx
from *Whatever Works:*

   1 large copper lined skillet,
                non stick
   12 small clear containers
                to hold batteries
   2 plastic containers to hold
                plastic wrap
   1 blue cushion with arms
                to soften a chair
   1 flashlight that beams
                dim to bright
   3 packs of magnet clasps
                (for me, he said,
                to extend necklaces)
   1 spiral notebook
                to note special days
   1 spiral notebook
                to note internet passwords
   1 large notebook to document
                *Facts My Family Should Know*

In each shirt pocket he stores small flashlights
imprinted with his name.

This morning he woke at 2 a.m.
insisting on breakfast. No dearth
for him. No darkness.

# Grandson

*Grandpa can't die, no, he can't!*
*I can help him, I'm near*
*at school, only one subway*
*away from the hospital where*

*he's in the ICU. I try to hold him*
*close, his kind of bear hug,*
*and he smiles, and I will*
*not let him die. I look up*

*death on the internet; it gives*
*me Jesus. He did not die!*
*All that is news*
*to me and I'm excited—*

*Jesus never died because*
*he was a good man and Grandpa*
*is a good man. I text*
*the Rabbi, the one who taught me*

*to be a man,*
*who said it's good to ask questions.*
*Now he wants me to understand*
*grandpa's wish to be*

*at peace. My job is to love him*
*wherever he is.*
                    *At the cemetery*
*I say the Kaddish*
*and take the shovel*
*to cover him with earth.*

# Elegiac Couplets

This is the house that Jack built.
This is the maiden who lived in the house that

Jack and Jill climbed up the hill
To fetch a pail. Jack fell.

It was the day of the eclipse
The sun disappeared as if

Where is the boy
Who looks after the sheep?

Moved to another bed
Fast asleep.

When the blazing sun is gone
When he nothing shines upon

We couldn't see, we couldn't look.
The mouse ran up the clock...

*Our* and *we* belong to us,
*I* remains when *we* is dust.

# Dearth

Decapitation enters
my dream. *Speak*
becomes *peak, dear*
*ear* and *swords* give me

*words.* In winter death
wiped my mate away—
ate him in a way. The head
of the house he was called.

Dreams uproot to make things new,
the future tense: September,
the New Year. *Listen, witness*
*how it is to be done.*

How it is to be one.

# These Are the Pearls

It's *Besame Mucho* coming through
revolving doors. It's 2018, the future
far from songs we danced to
left inside me. A waiter stands
to take my order.
                              O waiter,
bring me fresh plums on a plate.

He'd refuse to eat. Patiently,
his caretaker urged, "We want you
to be well; if you won't eat, she'll kill me."
He smiled, "Then we'll have to go to your funeral."
He could do that—Southern charmer
to the end.

To find him open the kitchen cabinet:
Coca-Cola, a bag of Cheetos,
the salt inside the shaker he would fill;
a half jar of Skippy peanut butter
still intact. I don't want it.
                              It's more than I can fathom!—
the whole of the kitchen. The future
filled with *Besame Mucho* and blintzes
he stored in the freezer.

Thaw little pancakes . . .
Flicker flicker . . .
I am speaking of his flashlights in the drawer.

# Fall and Spring

*—with gratitude for Gerard Manley Hopkins*

In our house we're grieving
Over golden boy who's leaving
Us to taxes, bank accounts,
The hanging ties. The world
In Tweets and counterfeit.
How to imagine it? This
By and by
He would not sigh for.
Spared the sorrow
Of his optimism gone
Awry, he leaves
The living to repair
The world he cared for. Can we?

# Knee

When I was twenty I replaced
My birth name (called paternal)

With another's. Nee Stein I'd been—
Shapiro would erase it. The maiden

Miss became a Mrs. proud to be
So consummately addressed.

As a wife, appointments held authority;
Say *Mrs.* and you surely had a life.

At thirty-five I suddenly became a Ms
Free to dwell in Dickinson's possibilities,

To hold an MA which meant I could
Be master of the arts, placing children elsewhere

While I earned it. The world walked toward me,
Consciousness for a life in NYC—lover of

Words, my own
Upright on a page.

A life that fit.

At 84, a widow, my knee
Is out of joint. I will replace it.

# Thwack

Leaving my New York apartment, going out
to Union Square, I'm headed for the park.
I've been reading poems, and a phrase
sticks—something about thwacking trees
spurs me on—toward my childhood?
Toward 80 years ago
                                    the lone kid
the fighter when the only way
the only way
to be seen was belonging
to myself.

I had to learn how to play
in a rich mix of marriage, children,
graduate degrees, reading,
writing to be the one in front
of the class, a teacher—conducting—
up on the strings, down on the horns.
Now my husband wants
                            me to join him
                            beneath a hanging spruce.

It's rising—the urge to thwack it.

# Borscht

Buy a marrowbone for stock,
add fresh beets, onion, carrots,
throw in lima beans,
simmer for three hours, then
serve it to your family.

When everyone has eaten,
leaving you to eat alone,
linger—close your eyes, take
the bone into your hands
to chew the clinging bits of meat

until the bone is smooth as ivory, and,
having saved the best for last,
rough your lips along its porous edge to
suck—deep, precise—
a hummingbird's exacting tongue. The quivering

marrow will be yours, earth's
sweet offering: the butcher, the broth,
the bone, and solitude.

When I leave this earth I want to be that very bone
used up for all I'm worth.

# Duvet

Words are the blanket on my bed.

Sheep and ducks gave up their coats for me.

Traveling backroads, sleep

Gave up dreams for me
                        to under stand
How warm the world can be.

# The Dispatcher's Waltz

*Step Back*

She was wild. No curfew. Climbed out second-story windows
      from her Texas U. dorm
            for a late date with the best dancer.
He wanted to go far—he would dip, she allowed him
      first base in the backseat of a car
            but only next day in broad daylight.

*Forward*

The tall windows of their New York apartment, 12 floors up
      go almost floor to ceiling
            hazy after many years of going.
Children ask for clarity. What's up? Difficult these days
      the steps to the roof
            where flowers bloom.

*Back*

Gardenias. A corsage of orchids, if you mattered.
      From the one who
            sent poems: "Ah, love, let us be true to. . ."
Barton Springs. Grill the meat, make a fire.
      spread the blanket—.
            wild was his rolling over

*Forward*

Rules. He doesn't want a senior residence, even if he could hear
      the piano player sing
            *You're the top* at teatime.
Where the deer and the antelope play
      is more like it.

*Pause*

I am she. I wanted to be wild. I will be.
   There's a bed on a hilltop
      where he'll lie next to me

as I climb over and under
    to an old flame
      John Garfield *(Body and Soul),*
and he, the dipper, will twist
    with Judy Holiday,
      the Gershwins nearby.
See if you can find me. Read Whitman. Take the train to
    Hastings-on-Hudson. Climb the hill, and
      when you leave there's cappuccino at the station.

# About the Author

Myra Shapiro, born in the Bronx, returned to New York City after forty-five years in Georgia and Tennessee where she married Harold Shapiro, raised two daughters and worked as a teacher and librarian. She holds a BA in American Literature (University of Chattanooga), MA in English (Bread Loaf School of English, Middlebury College) and MFA in Writing (Vermont College). She received the Dylan Thomas Poetry Award from The New School and was a finalist for the Robert H. Winner Award from the Poetry Society of America. She has held fellowships at the Banff Arts Center, MacDowell Colony (twice), and Hedgebrook.

Shapiro's books of poetry are *I'll See You Thursday* and *12 Floors Above the Earth,* her memoir, *Four Sublets: Becoming a Poet in New York.* Her poems have appeared in many periodicals and anthologies, most recently *The New Yorker,* and twice, in *Best American Poetry.* She serves on the Board of Directors of Poets House and teaches poetry workshops for the International Women's Writing Guild.

www.ingramcontent.com/pod-product-compliance
Lightning Source LLC
Chambersburg PA
CBHW031149090426
42738CB00008B/1272